Animal C

by Luana K. Mitten and Mary M. Wagner

Contents

ROURKE CLASSROOM RESOURCES
The path to student success

Every animal has a **cover.**

Fur and Hair

Look at the rabbit's white fur.
It **camouflages** the rabbit
in the snow.

Look at the sheep's wooly fur.

Farmers shear sheep's wooly fur. We can make warm sweaters from the wool.

Look at the pig's hairy skin. The hair
is removed when we make leather from
pig skin.

Look at the dolphin's smooth skin.
The dolphin's skin helps it swim very fast.

Feathers

Look at the bird's brown and white feathers. The colors of the feathers camouflage the bird in the winter woods.

Look at the flamingos' pink feathers.
Did you know flamingos' feathers turn
pink because flamingos eat shrimp?

Scales and Shells

Look at the snake's green **scales**.
The snake's scales help it hide
and slide in the grass.

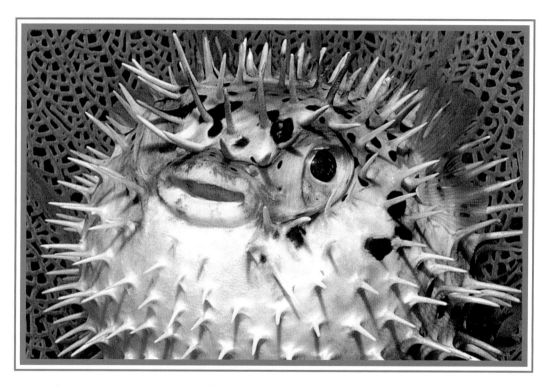

Look at the pufferfish's pointy scales.
When it puffs up **predators** stay away.

Look at the sea turtle's shell. The shell protects the turtle from predators.

Look at the snail's shell. The hard shell protects the snail's soft body.

Look at the ladybug's spotted wings.
They are hard like a shell.

Quills

Look at the porcupine's **quills** standing up. You better not touch them or you might get a quill in YOUR covering!

Animal Covers

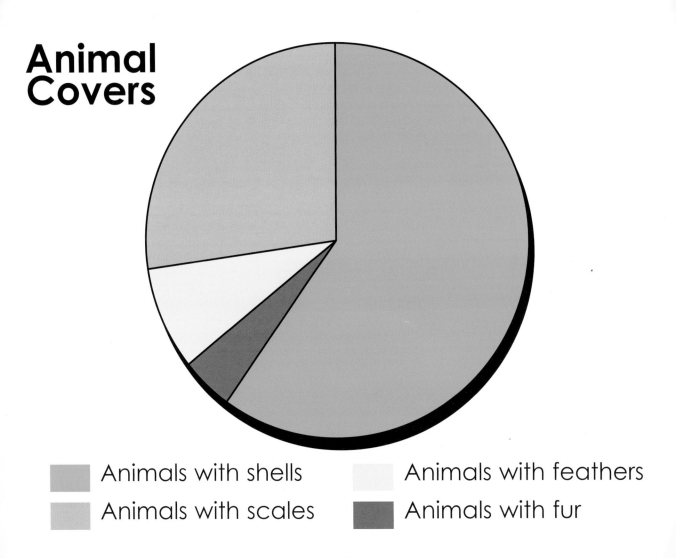

Animals with shells

Animals with feathers

Animals with scales

Animals with fur